# Chapters

# Chapter 1: Introduction

Artificial Intelligence (AI) is a rapidly growing field that has the potential to revolutionize the way we live our lives. From healthcare to education, transportation to entertainment, AI is already making its mark on various aspects of our daily lives. AI-powered systems can now diagnose medical conditions, drive cars, recommend movies, and even generate music.

As AI technology continues to advance, it will have an increasingly profound impact on our personal lives. From improving the quality of healthcare to optimizing our daily routines, AI has the potential to make our lives more convenient, efficient, and productive.

However, AI also raises important ethical questions about privacy, bias, and the role of human decision-making. As we continue to integrate AI into our personal lives, we must be aware of the potential risks and challenges.

This book explores the various ways in which AI is already changing our personal lives and how it will continue to shape our future. We will examine the impact of AI on healthcare, fitness, education, home automation, entertainment, transportation, finance, employment, communication, social media, shopping, travel, mental health, aging, food, environment, sports, and personal productivity.

We will also explore the ethical considerations that arise as AI becomes more integrated into our lives. By the end of this book, readers will have a deeper understanding of how AI is transforming our personal lives and what the future of AI might look like.

## The basics of AI and how it works

AI, or artificial intelligence, is a branch of computer science that focuses on creating machines that can perform tasks that would typically require human intelligence to complete. AI systems are designed to learn from data and improve their performance over time through a process known as machine learning.

The fundamental components of AI include:

Data: The foundation of any AI system is data. AI systems require large amounts of data to train and improve their performance.

Algorithms: AI systems use algorithms to process data and make decisions. These algorithms are designed to learn and improve their performance over time.

Models: AI systems use models to represent the knowledge they have acquired through the training process. These models can be used to make predictions, classify data, or perform other tasks.

Feedback: AI systems rely on feedback to improve their performance. Feedback can come in the form of new data, user input, or other forms of interaction with the system.

AI systems can be divided into two broad categories: narrow AI and general AI. Narrow AI systems are designed to perform specific tasks, such as recognizing speech or identifying objects in images. General AI systems, on the other hand, are designed to perform a wide range of tasks and exhibit human-like intelligence.

In order to create AI systems, developers typically use programming languages such as Python or Java, as well as specialized AI frameworks and libraries. These tools enable developers to build and train AI systems more efficiently, allowing them to create more advanced and sophisticated AI applications.

Overall, AI is a rapidly advancing field that has the potential to transform the way we live our lives. As AI technology continues to improve, we can expect to see more and more AI systems that are capable of performing tasks that were previously thought to be impossible for machines.

## The impact of AI on personal lives

The impact of AI on personal lives is already significant and will continue to grow in the coming years. AI-powered systems are changing the way we interact with technology, and they are enabling new levels of convenience, efficiency, and productivity.

One area where AI is having a significant impact is healthcare. AI-powered systems are being used to diagnose medical conditions, design personalized treatment plans, and even perform surgeries. AI-powered medical devices are also being developed to help patients monitor their health and manage chronic conditions.

AI is also changing the way we stay fit and healthy. AI-powered fitness trackers and apps are enabling people to monitor their physical activity, track their nutrition, and receive personalized workout plans. AI-assisted virtual coaching is also becoming more common, allowing people to receive guidance and support from fitness experts without leaving their homes.

In education, AI is being used to personalize learning and improve student outcomes. AI-powered tools and technologies are being developed to assist teachers in grading assignments, identifying areas where students may need extra help, and even creating personalized lesson plans based on each student's strengths and weaknesses.

In home automation, AI-powered smart home systems are becoming more popular, allowing people to control their home environment with voice commands or a smartphone app. AI-powered energy management systems are also being developed to help people save money on their utility bills and reduce their environmental impact.

AI is also changing the way we consume entertainment. AI-powered recommendation systems are being used to suggest movies, TV shows, and music that we are likely to enjoy. AI-assisted video game development is also becoming more common, allowing developers to create more engaging and immersive gaming experiences.

Overall, the impact of AI on personal lives is already significant and will continue to grow in the coming years. While AI has the potential to bring many benefits to our lives, there are also important ethical considerations that must be addressed as AI technology continues to advance.

# Chapter 2: Healthcare

One of the most promising areas of application for AI is healthcare. AI-powered systems have the potential to transform the way we diagnose, treat, and prevent diseases, as well as manage our overall health and wellbeing.

In recent years, AI-powered medical diagnosis has shown great promise. AI systems can analyze vast amounts of medical data, including patient history, lab results, and imaging scans, to help doctors make more accurate diagnoses. AI systems are also being used to develop personalized treatment plans based on a patient's unique medical profile.

AI-powered medical devices are also being developed to help patients monitor their health and manage chronic conditions. For example, AI-powered wearables can track a patient's heart rate, blood pressure, and other vital signs, providing real-time data that can be used to identify potential health issues before they become serious.

AI is also being used to improve the drug development process. AI-powered systems can analyze large amounts of data to identify potential drug candidates, predict their efficacy and toxicity, and even design new molecules that could be used as drugs.

In this chapter, we will explore the various ways in which AI is already transforming healthcare and the potential for future developments in the field. We will examine the impact of AI on medical diagnosis, personalized treatment, medical devices, drug development, and more.

We will also discuss the ethical considerations that arise as AI becomes more integrated into healthcare. While AI has the potential to bring many benefits to patients and healthcare providers, there are also important concerns around patient privacy, data security, and the role of human decision-making.

Overall, AI is poised to revolutionize the healthcare industry, enabling better patient outcomes, improved efficiency, and lower costs. As AI technology continues to advance, we can expect to see even more innovative applications of AI in healthcare that will benefit patients around the world.

## AI-powered medical diagnosis

AI-powered medical diagnosis has shown great potential to revolutionize the way doctors diagnose and treat diseases. With the ability to analyze large amounts of medical data, including patient history, lab results, and imaging scans, AI systems can assist doctors in making more accurate and efficient diagnoses.

One example of AI-powered medical diagnosis is in the field of radiology. AI systems can analyze medical images such as X-rays, CT scans, and MRIs to identify potential abnormalities and assist radiologists in making more accurate diagnoses. AI-powered systems can also help radiologists detect early signs of diseases, such as cancer, before they become visible on traditional medical imaging.

AI-powered medical diagnosis is also being used to improve the accuracy of cancer diagnoses. AI systems can analyze tumor samples and provide doctors with information about the type and stage of the cancer. This can help doctors develop personalized treatment plans that are tailored to each patient's specific needs.

In addition to improving the accuracy of medical diagnosis, AI-powered systems can also help doctors identify potential health risks before they become serious. For example, AI-powered wearable devices can track a patient's vital signs and provide early warning signs of potential health issues.

While AI-powered medical diagnosis has the potential to bring many benefits to patients and healthcare providers, there are also important ethical considerations that must be addressed. These include concerns around patient privacy, data security, and the role of human decision-making in medical diagnosis.

Overall, AI-powered medical diagnosis is a rapidly advancing field that has the potential to revolutionize the way doctors diagnose and treat diseases. As AI technology continues to improve, we can expect to see even more innovative applications of AI in medical diagnosis that will benefit patients around the world.

## AI-assisted surgeries

AI-assisted surgeries are another area where AI technology is transforming the healthcare industry. AI systems can assist surgeons in performing complex surgical procedures by providing real-time guidance and feedback.

One example of AI-assisted surgery is the use of robotic surgical systems. These systems use AI-powered algorithms to control robotic arms that are used to perform minimally invasive surgeries. The surgeon controls the robotic arms using a console, and the AI system provides real-time feedback to ensure that the surgery is performed accurately and safely.

AI-assisted surgeries can also help reduce the risk of complications and improve patient outcomes. For example, AI systems can help surgeons identify potential blood vessels and nerves that could be damaged during surgery, and they can also help surgeons perform more precise and accurate incisions.

In addition to improving surgical accuracy, AI-assisted surgeries can also help reduce the length of hospital stays and recovery times. This can help reduce healthcare costs and improve patient satisfaction.

However, there are also important ethical considerations that must be addressed when using AI in surgery. These include concerns around patient safety, privacy, and the role of human decision-making in surgery.

Overall, AI-assisted surgeries are a rapidly advancing field that has the potential to transform the way surgeries are performed. As AI technology continues to improve, we can expect to see even more innovative applications of AI in surgery that will benefit patients around the world.

## AI-driven drug development

AI-driven drug development is another area where AI technology is transforming the healthcare industry. Developing new drugs is a complex and time-consuming process that involves extensive research, testing, and regulatory approval. AI-powered systems can accelerate this process by analyzing vast amounts of data and identifying potential drug candidates that would be difficult for humans to find.

One example of AI-driven drug development is the use of AI-powered algorithms to analyze medical data and identify potential drug candidates. AI systems can analyze large amounts of medical data, including patient records, genetic data, and clinical trial results, to identify potential drug targets and predict the effectiveness of new drugs.

AI is also being used to design new molecules that could be used as drugs. AI systems can analyze the structure and properties of existing molecules to identify potential candidates for drug development. They can also design new molecules that have specific properties that would be useful in drug development.

In addition to accelerating the drug development process, AI-driven drug development can also help reduce the costs associated with drug development. By identifying potential drug candidates more efficiently and accurately, AI-powered systems can help pharmaceutical companies reduce the amount of time and resources required to bring new drugs to market.

However, there are also important ethical considerations that must be addressed when using AI in drug development. These include concerns around patient safety, data privacy, and the role of human decision-making in drug development.

Overall, AI-driven drug development is a rapidly advancing field that has the potential to revolutionize the way new drugs are developed and brought to market. As AI technology continues to improve, we can expect to see even more innovative applications of AI in drug development that will benefit patients around the world.

# Chapter 3: Fitness

Fitness is an area where AI technology is having a significant impact on personal lives. AI-powered fitness tools and technologies are enabling people to monitor their physical activity, track their nutrition, and receive personalized workout plans.

AI-powered fitness tracking has become increasingly popular in recent years. Wearable devices, such as fitness trackers and smartwatches, can monitor a person's physical activity, heart rate, and other vital signs. This data can be analyzed by AI-powered algorithms to provide insights into a person's fitness levels and help them make adjustments to their workouts.

AI-powered personalized workout plans are also becoming more common. AI systems can analyze a person's fitness data and provide personalized workout plans based on their goals, fitness level, and preferences. AI-assisted virtual coaching is also becoming more popular, allowing people to receive guidance and support from fitness experts without leaving their homes.

AI is also being used to track nutrition and provide personalized meal plans. AI systems can analyze a person's diet and provide recommendations for healthy foods and meal plans that are tailored to their individual needs.

In this chapter, we will explore the various ways in which AI is transforming the fitness industry and how it is enabling people to improve their physical health and wellbeing. We will examine the impact of AI on fitness tracking, personalized workout plans, virtual coaching, nutrition tracking, and more.

We will also discuss the ethical considerations that arise as AI becomes more integrated into fitness. While AI has the potential to bring many benefits to fitness enthusiasts, there are also concerns around data privacy, algorithmic bias, and the role of human decision-making in fitness.

Overall, AI-powered fitness tools and technologies are making it easier for people to monitor their physical activity, track their nutrition, and receive personalized workout plans. As AI technology continues to improve, we can expect to see even more innovative applications of AI in fitness that will benefit people around the world.

## AI-powered fitness tracking

AI-powered fitness tracking is a rapidly growing area that is changing the way people monitor their physical activity and fitness levels. With the help of wearable devices, such as fitness trackers and smartwatches, people can now collect vast amounts of data about their physical activity, heart rate, and other vital signs. AI-powered algorithms can then analyze this data to provide insights into a person's fitness level and offer recommendations for improving their health and fitness.

One example of AI-powered fitness tracking is the use of wearable devices that track a person's physical activity throughout the day. These devices can collect data on a person's steps taken, distance traveled, and calories burned. AI-powered algorithms can then analyze this data to provide insights into a person's fitness level and make recommendations for achieving fitness goals.

AI-powered fitness tracking can also help people monitor their heart rate and other vital signs during exercise. Wearable devices can track a person's heart rate and provide real-time feedback on their exercise intensity. AI-powered algorithms can then analyze this data to provide insights into a person's fitness level and make recommendations for achieving their fitness goals.

In addition to monitoring physical activity, AI-powered fitness tracking can also provide insights into a person's sleep patterns. Wearable devices can track a person's sleep quality and duration, and AI-powered algorithms can analyze this data to provide insights into a person's overall health and wellbeing.

While AI-powered fitness tracking has the potential to bring many benefits to people looking to improve their health and fitness, there are also important ethical considerations that must be addressed. These include concerns around data privacy, algorithmic bias, and the role of human decision-making in fitness.

Overall, AI-powered fitness tracking is a rapidly advancing field that has the potential to revolutionize the way people monitor their physical activity and fitness levels. As AI technology continues to improve, we can expect to see even more innovative applications of AI in fitness tracking that will benefit people around the world.

## AI-based personalized workout plans

AI-based personalized workout plans are another area where AI technology is transforming the fitness industry. AI-powered algorithms can analyze a person's fitness data and provide personalized workout plans that are tailored to their goals, fitness level, and preferences.

One example of AI-based personalized workout plans is the use of AI-powered fitness apps. These apps can collect data on a person's physical activity, heart rate, and other vital signs and use this data to provide personalized workout plans. AI algorithms can also analyze a person's workout data to provide feedback on their exercise intensity and make recommendations for achieving their fitness goals.

AI-based virtual coaching is also becoming more popular. With the help of AI-powered algorithms, fitness coaches can provide personalized workout plans and advice to clients remotely. This allows people to receive guidance and support from fitness experts without leaving their homes.

AI-powered personalized workout plans can also help people avoid injury and improve their exercise technique. AI algorithms can analyze a person's workout data to provide feedback on their form and offer recommendations for making adjustments to their workouts.

While AI-based personalized workout plans have the potential to bring many benefits to people looking to improve their health and fitness, there are also important ethical considerations that must be addressed. These include concerns around data privacy, algorithmic bias, and the role of human decision-making in fitness.

Overall, AI-based personalized workout plans are a rapidly advancing field that has the potential to revolutionize the way people approach their fitness goals. As AI technology continues to improve, we can expect to see even more innovative applications of AI in personalized workout plans that will benefit people around the world.

## AI-assisted virtual coaching

AI-assisted virtual coaching is a rapidly growing field in the fitness industry. With the help of AI-powered algorithms, fitness coaches can provide personalized workout plans and advice to clients remotely. This allows people to receive guidance and support from fitness experts without leaving their homes.

One example of AI-assisted virtual coaching is the use of AI-powered fitness apps. These apps can collect data on a person's physical activity, heart rate, and other vital signs and use this data to provide personalized workout plans. AI algorithms can also analyze a person's workout data to provide feedback on their exercise intensity and make recommendations for achieving their fitness goals. With the help of AI, fitness coaches can customize the workout plans and provide feedback based on the person's data and preferences.

AI-assisted virtual coaching can also provide people with motivation and accountability. With regular check-ins and feedback from the fitness coach, people are more likely to stay on track with their fitness goals.

In addition to improving the quality of virtual coaching, AI algorithms can also help automate administrative tasks, such as scheduling and billing. This allows coaches to spend more time working with clients and less time on administrative tasks.

While AI-assisted virtual coaching has the potential to bring many benefits to people looking to improve their health and fitness, there are also important ethical considerations that must be addressed. These include concerns around data privacy, algorithmic bias, and the role of human decision-making in fitness coaching.

Overall, AI-assisted virtual coaching is a rapidly advancing field that has the potential to revolutionize the way people approach their fitness goals. As AI technology continues to improve, we can expect to see even more innovative applications of AI in virtual coaching that will benefit people around the world.

# Chapter 4: Education

AI is transforming the field of education by providing new tools and technologies that are making it easier for students to learn and educators to teach. AI-powered systems can analyze vast amounts of data, personalize learning experiences, and provide real-time feedback to students and teachers.

AI is being used to improve student learning outcomes in a variety of ways. For example, AI-powered systems can provide personalized learning experiences that are tailored to each student's unique needs and learning style. These systems can analyze a student's performance data to identify areas where they need additional support and provide targeted recommendations for improvement.

AI-powered systems can also help educators develop more effective teaching strategies. By analyzing student performance data, AI systems can identify patterns and trends that can inform instructional decisions. AI-powered systems can also provide real-time feedback to teachers, helping them adjust their teaching strategies to better meet the needs of their students.

In addition to improving student learning outcomes, AI is also being used to improve accessibility and equity in education. AI-powered systems can provide language translation services and assistive technologies to students with disabilities, allowing them to participate in the learning process more effectively.

In this chapter, we will explore the various ways in which AI is transforming the field of education and how it is enabling students and educators to achieve better learning outcomes. We will examine the impact of AI on personalized learning, teacher support, accessibility and equity, and more.

We will also discuss the ethical considerations that arise as AI becomes more integrated into education. While AI has the potential to bring many benefits to students and educators, there are also concerns around data privacy, algorithmic bias, and the role of human decision-making in education.

Overall, AI-powered systems are making it easier for students to learn and educators to teach. As AI technology continues to improve, we can expect to see even more innovative applications of AI in education that will benefit students around the world.

## AI-powered personalized learning

AI-powered personalized learning is a rapidly growing field that is changing the way students learn. With the help of AI-powered algorithms, personalized learning experiences can be tailored to each student's unique needs and learning style.

One example of AI-powered personalized learning is the use of adaptive learning systems. These systems use AI algorithms to analyze a student's performance data and provide personalized learning recommendations based on their strengths and weaknesses. The system can then adjust the difficulty of the learning material based on the student's progress, ensuring that they are challenged but not overwhelmed.

AI-powered personalized learning can also provide students with real-time feedback. AI algorithms can analyze a student's work and provide feedback on their performance, highlighting areas where they need additional support and providing recommendations for improvement.

AI-powered personalized learning can also provide students with a more engaging learning experience. AI-powered systems can use gamification and other interactive elements to make learning more fun and rewarding.

While AI-powered personalized learning has the potential to bring many benefits to students, there are also important ethical considerations that must be addressed. These include concerns around data privacy, algorithmic bias, and the role of human decision-making in education.

Overall, AI-powered personalized learning is a rapidly advancing field that has the potential to revolutionize the way students learn. As AI technology continues to improve, we can expect to see even more innovative applications of AI in personalized learning that will benefit students around the world.

## AI-based assessment and grading

AI-based assessment and grading is another area where AI technology is transforming the field of education. AI algorithms can analyze student work and provide automated assessments and grading, saving teachers time and ensuring more objective evaluations.

One example of AI-based assessment and grading is the use of automated essay grading systems. AI algorithms can analyze a student's written work and provide feedback on grammar, structure, and other aspects of the writing. The system can also provide a score for the essay, based on factors such as organization and coherence.

AI-based assessment and grading can also be used for multiple-choice questions and other types of assessments. AI algorithms can analyze student responses and provide immediate feedback on their performance. This can help students identify areas where they need additional support and help teachers identify areas where they need to adjust their instructional strategies.

In addition to saving time and improving objectivity, AI-based assessment and grading can also help improve accessibility and equity in education. By providing immediate feedback, students can receive more support and guidance, regardless of their geographical location or socio-economic background.

While AI-based assessment and grading has the potential to bring many benefits to students and educators, there are also important ethical considerations that must be addressed. These include concerns around data privacy, algorithmic bias, and the role of human decision-making in education.

Overall, AI-based assessment and grading is a rapidly advancing field that has the potential to revolutionize the way student work is evaluated. As AI technology continues to improve, we can expect to see even more innovative applications of AI in assessment and grading that will benefit students and educators around the world.

## AI-driven educational tools and technologies

AI-driven educational tools and technologies are transforming the field of education by providing new ways for students to learn and teachers to teach. These tools and technologies are enabling personalized learning experiences, providing real-time feedback, and improving accessibility and equity in education.

One example of AI-driven educational tools and technologies is the use of intelligent tutoring systems. These systems use AI algorithms to analyze a student's performance data and provide personalized recommendations for improvement. The system can also adjust the difficulty of the learning material based on the student's progress, ensuring that they are challenged but not overwhelmed.

AI-driven educational tools and technologies can also provide real-time feedback to students and teachers. For example, AI algorithms can analyze student work and provide immediate feedback on their performance, allowing students to identify areas where they need additional support and teachers to adjust their instructional strategies.

AI-driven educational tools and technologies can also help improve accessibility and equity in education. For example, AI-powered translation services can provide language support to students who speak different languages, and assistive technologies can provide support to students with disabilities.

While AI-driven educational tools and technologies have the potential to bring many benefits to students and educators, there are also important ethical considerations that must be addressed. These include concerns around data privacy, algorithmic bias, and the role of human decision-making in education.

Overall, AI-driven educational tools and technologies are a rapidly advancing field that has the potential to revolutionize the way students learn and teachers teach. As AI technology continues to improve, we can expect to see even more innovative applications of AI in education that will benefit students and educators around the world.

# Chapter 5: Home Automation

Home automation is an area where AI technology is rapidly transforming our personal lives. With the help of AI-powered systems, people can control various aspects of their homes, such as lighting, heating, and security, with just a few taps on their smartphones.

AI-powered home automation systems use sensors, cameras, and other devices to collect data about a person's home environment. AI algorithms can then analyze this data to provide insights into a person's energy usage, security risks, and more. This allows people to make more informed decisions about how to manage their homes and conserve energy.

AI-powered home automation systems can also provide real-time alerts and notifications to homeowners. For example, if a security camera detects unusual activity, an AI system can send an alert to the homeowner's smartphone. Similarly, if a home's temperature is outside of the desired range, an AI system can adjust the heating or cooling settings to bring the temperature back to a comfortable level.

In addition to improving convenience and security, AI-powered home automation systems can also help people save money on their energy bills. By monitoring energy usage and making adjustments to heating, cooling, and lighting settings, AI systems can help homeowners reduce their energy consumption and save money on their energy bills.

In this chapter, we will explore the various ways in which AI is transforming the field of home automation and how it is enabling people to live more comfortably, safely, and efficiently. We will examine the impact of AI on lighting, heating, security, and more.

We will also discuss the ethical considerations that arise as AI becomes more integrated into home automation. While AI has the potential to bring many benefits to homeowners, there are also concerns around data privacy, algorithmic bias, and the role of human decision-making in home automation.

Overall, AI-powered home automation systems are making it easier for people to control various aspects of their homes and live more comfortably and efficiently. As AI technology continues to improve, we can expect to see even more innovative applications of AI in home automation that will benefit homeowners around the world.

**AI-powered smart homes**

AI-powered smart homes are a rapidly growing area that is changing the way people interact with their homes. With the help of AI-powered systems, people can control various aspects of their homes, such as lighting, heating, and security, with just a few taps on their smartphones.

One example of AI-powered smart homes is the use of voice-activated assistants, such as Amazon's Alexa or Google Home. These devices use AI algorithms to interpret a person's voice commands and control various aspects of their home, such as turning on lights, adjusting the thermostat, and playing music.

AI-powered smart homes can also be used for security purposes. For example, AI-powered security cameras can analyze footage in real-time and alert homeowners to any unusual activity. Similarly, AI algorithms can analyze data from various sensors and alert homeowners to potential safety hazards, such as smoke or carbon monoxide.

AI-powered smart homes can also help people conserve energy and reduce their carbon footprint. By monitoring energy usage and making adjustments to heating, cooling, and lighting settings, AI systems can help homeowners reduce their energy consumption and save money on their energy bills.

While AI-powered smart homes have the potential to bring many benefits to homeowners, there are also important ethical considerations that must be addressed. These include concerns around data privacy, algorithmic bias, and the role of human decision-making in home automation.

Overall, AI-powered smart homes are a rapidly advancing field that has the potential to revolutionize the way people interact with their homes. As AI technology continues to improve, we can expect to see even more innovative applications of AI in smart homes that will benefit homeowners around the world.

## AI-based energy management

AI-based energy management is another area where AI technology is transforming the field of home automation. AI algorithms can analyze data from various sensors and devices to provide insights into a person's energy usage and make recommendations for reducing energy consumption.

AI-based energy management can help people save money on their energy bills and reduce their carbon footprint. By analyzing data from various sensors and devices, AI algorithms can identify areas where energy consumption can be reduced, such as adjusting the thermostat, turning off lights and electronics when not in use, and using energy-efficient appliances.

AI-based energy management can also provide real-time alerts and notifications to homeowners. For example, if a home's energy consumption is higher than usual, an AI system can send an alert to the homeowner's smartphone and provide recommendations for reducing energy usage.

In addition to improving energy efficiency, AI-based energy management can also help homeowners integrate renewable energy sources into their homes. For example, an AI system can analyze data from solar panels and battery storage systems to optimize energy usage and maximize the use of renewable energy sources.

While AI-based energy management has the potential to bring many benefits to homeowners, there are also important ethical considerations that must be addressed. These include concerns around data privacy, algorithmic bias, and the role of human decision-making in energy management.

Overall, AI-based energy management is a rapidly advancing field that has the potential to revolutionize the way people manage their energy usage. As AI technology continues to improve, we can expect to see even more innovative applications of AI in energy management that will benefit homeowners around the world.

## AI-driven security systems

AI-driven security systems are a rapidly growing area of home automation that is changing the way people protect their homes. With the help of AI-powered algorithms, security systems can provide real-time monitoring and alerts, improving the safety and security of homes.

One example of AI-driven security systems is the use of security cameras with AI algorithms. These cameras can analyze footage in real-time and provide alerts when unusual activity is detected. For example, an AI-powered security camera can detect when a person is loitering outside a home or when a package is delivered to the front porch.

AI-driven security systems can also be used to improve access control. For example, AI algorithms can analyze data from smart locks and provide alerts when someone enters the home without authorization. Similarly, AI algorithms can analyze data from sensors and provide alerts when doors or windows are left open.

AI-driven security systems can also be integrated with other home automation systems, such as lighting and heating, to provide an additional layer of security. For example, an AI system can turn on lights or adjust the thermostat to make it appear as though someone is home, even when the homeowner is away.

While AI-driven security systems have the potential to bring many benefits to homeowners, there are also important ethical considerations that must be addressed. These include concerns around data privacy, algorithmic bias, and the role of human decision-making in security systems.

Overall, AI-driven security systems are a rapidly advancing field that has the potential to revolutionize the way people protect their homes. As AI technology continues to improve, we can expect to see even more innovative applications of AI in security systems that will benefit homeowners around the world.

# Chapter 6: Entertainment

AI technology is transforming the field of entertainment, providing new ways for people to consume and interact with media. AI-powered systems can personalize recommendations, create new content, and improve the overall entertainment experience.

AI-powered systems can analyze a person's viewing and listening habits and provide personalized recommendations for movies, TV shows, music, and podcasts. This allows people to discover new content that is tailored to their unique interests and preferences.

AI-powered systems can also be used to create new content. For example, AI algorithms can analyze data from social media and other sources to generate new ideas for TV shows, movies, and other forms of media. AI-powered systems can also be used to enhance the quality of existing content, such as by improving the visual effects or sound quality of a movie or TV show.

AI-powered systems can also be used to improve the overall entertainment experience. For example, AI algorithms can analyze data from a person's viewing or listening habits to provide real-time recommendations for what to watch or listen to next. AI-powered systems can also analyze data from various sensors and devices to create immersive experiences, such as augmented reality or virtual reality experiences.

In this chapter, we will explore the various ways in which AI is transforming the field of entertainment and how it is enabling people to consume and interact with media in new ways. We will examine the impact of AI on personalized recommendations, content creation, immersive experiences, and more.

We will also discuss the ethical considerations that arise as AI becomes more integrated into entertainment. While AI has the potential to bring many benefits to consumers and content creators, there are also concerns around data privacy, algorithmic bias, and the role of human decision-making in entertainment.

Overall, AI-powered systems are changing the way people consume and interact with media, providing new ways for people to discover content and enhancing the overall entertainment experience. As AI technology continues to improve, we can expect to see even more innovative applications of AI in entertainment that will benefit consumers and content creators around the world.

## AI-powered movie recommendations

AI-powered movie recommendations are a rapidly growing area of entertainment that is changing the way people discover new movies and TV shows. With the help of AI-powered algorithms, personalized recommendations can be tailored to each person's unique interests and preferences.

AI algorithms can analyze a person's viewing habits, preferences, and other data to create a personalized list of recommended movies and TV shows. The system can then adjust the recommendations based on a person's feedback, ensuring that the recommendations continue to be tailored to their interests.

AI-powered movie recommendations can also help people discover new content that they may not have otherwise found. By analyzing data from various sources, such as social media and movie review websites, AI algorithms can provide recommendations for movies and TV shows that are similar to those that a person has enjoyed in the past.

AI-powered movie recommendations can also help content creators by providing insights into what types of movies and TV shows are popular among certain audiences. By analyzing data on viewing habits and preferences, content creators can better understand what types of content to create and how to market it to specific audiences.

While AI-powered movie recommendations have the potential to bring many benefits to consumers and content creators, there are also important ethical considerations that must be addressed. These include concerns around data privacy, algorithmic bias, and the role of human decision-making in movie recommendations.

Overall, AI-powered movie recommendations are a rapidly advancing field that has the potential to revolutionize the way people discover new movies and TV shows. As AI technology continues to improve, we can expect to see even more innovative applications of AI in personalized movie recommendations that will benefit consumers and content creators around the world.

## AI-assisted video game development

AI-assisted video game development is a rapidly growing area of entertainment that is changing the way video games are created and played. With the help of AI-powered systems, game developers can create more immersive experiences, improve gameplay, and reduce development time.

AI algorithms can analyze data from various sources, such as player behavior and game telemetry, to provide insights into how players interact with games. This information can be used to improve game design, balance difficulty levels, and create more engaging gameplay experiences.

AI-powered systems can also be used to create more realistic and immersive worlds. For example, AI algorithms can analyze data from satellite imagery and other sources to create more realistic environments in open-world games. AI-powered systems can also be used to create more realistic characters and NPCs, improving the overall storytelling and gameplay experience.

AI-assisted game development can also help reduce development time and costs. For example, AI algorithms can generate terrain, textures, and other assets, reducing the need for human artists to create them manually. This can help game developers create more content in less time, allowing them to release games more quickly and at a lower cost.

While AI-assisted game development has the potential to bring many benefits to game developers and players, there are also important ethical considerations that must be addressed. These include concerns around data privacy, algorithmic bias, and the role of human decision-making in game development.

Overall, AI-assisted game development is a rapidly advancing field that has the potential to revolutionize the way video games are created and played. As AI technology continues to improve, we can expect to see even more innovative applications of AI in video game development that will benefit game developers and players around the world.

## AI-generated music

AI-generated music is a rapidly growing area of entertainment that is changing the way music is created and consumed. With the help of AI-powered systems, music can be generated and personalized to each listener's unique tastes.

AI algorithms can analyze data from various sources, such as a person's listening habits and preferences, to create personalized playlists and music recommendations. The system can also create new music based on a person's unique preferences and style.

AI-generated music can also be used to enhance the creative process for musicians and producers. For example, AI algorithms can analyze existing music and generate new melodies or chord progressions that are similar in style. This can help musicians and producers create new music more quickly and efficiently.

AI-generated music can also be used in other areas of entertainment, such as film and TV soundtracks. AI algorithms can analyze the mood and tone of a scene and generate music that complements the visual content.

While AI-generated music has the potential to bring many benefits to musicians and music lovers, there are also important ethical considerations that must be addressed. These include concerns around intellectual property rights, the role of human creativity in music, and the potential for algorithmic bias in music generation.

Overall, AI-generated music is a rapidly advancing field that has the potential to revolutionize the way music is created and consumed. As AI technology continues to improve, we can expect to see even more innovative applications of AI in music generation that will benefit musicians and music lovers around the world.

# Chapter 7: Transportation

AI technology is transforming the field of transportation, providing new ways to improve safety, efficiency, and sustainability. AI-powered systems can analyze data from various sensors and devices to optimize transportation systems, improve traffic flow, and reduce emissions.

In this chapter, we will explore the various ways in which AI is transforming transportation and how it is enabling people to travel more safely, efficiently, and sustainably. We will examine the impact of AI on autonomous vehicles, traffic management systems, and public transportation.

We will also discuss the ethical considerations that arise as AI becomes more integrated into transportation. While AI has the potential to bring many benefits to transportation systems and users, there are also concerns around data privacy, algorithmic bias, and the role of human decision-making in transportation.

Overall, AI-powered systems are changing the way people travel, providing new opportunities to improve safety, efficiency, and sustainability. As AI technology continues to improve, we can expect to see even more innovative applications of AI in transportation that will benefit individuals and communities around the world.

## AI-driven self-driving cars

AI-driven self-driving cars are a rapidly advancing area of transportation that is changing the way people travel. With the help of AI-powered systems, self-driving cars can safely navigate roads, avoid collisions, and optimize travel routes.

AI algorithms can analyze data from various sensors and devices, such as cameras and LIDAR, to create a detailed map of the car's surroundings. This information can be used to safely navigate the road, avoid obstacles, and make decisions in real-time.

AI-driven self-driving cars can also improve the efficiency and safety of transportation systems. By optimizing travel routes, self-driving cars can reduce congestion, save time, and reduce emissions. AI algorithms can also analyze data from various sources, such as weather and traffic patterns, to make real-time adjustments to travel routes.

AI-driven self-driving cars can also provide mobility for individuals who may not have access to traditional forms of transportation, such as people with disabilities or the elderly.

While AI-driven self-driving cars have the potential to bring many benefits to transportation systems and users, there are also important ethical considerations that must be addressed. These include concerns around data privacy, algorithmic bias, and the role of human decision-making in self-driving cars.

Overall, AI-driven self-driving cars are a rapidly advancing field that has the potential to revolutionize the way people travel. As AI technology continues to improve, we can expect to see even more innovative applications of AI in self-driving cars that will benefit individuals and communities around the world.

## AI-assisted traffic management

AI-assisted traffic management is a rapidly growing area of transportation that is changing the way traffic flows on roads and highways. With the help of AI-powered systems, traffic management can be optimized in real-time to reduce congestion and improve safety.

AI algorithms can analyze data from various sensors and devices, such as cameras and traffic sensors, to provide real-time insights into traffic flow. This information can be used to adjust traffic signals, optimize travel routes, and alert drivers to potential hazards.

AI-assisted traffic management can also improve the safety of transportation systems. By analyzing data on traffic patterns and accidents, AI algorithms can provide insights into potential hazards and make real-time adjustments to reduce the risk of collisions.

AI-assisted traffic management can also improve the efficiency of transportation systems. By optimizing traffic flow, reducing congestion, and minimizing delays, AI algorithms can save time and reduce emissions.

While AI-assisted traffic management has the potential to bring many benefits to transportation systems and users, there are also important ethical considerations that must be addressed. These include concerns around data privacy, algorithmic bias, and the role of human decision-making in traffic management.

Overall, AI-assisted traffic management is a rapidly advancing field that has the potential to revolutionize the way traffic flows on roads and highways. As AI technology continues to improve, we can expect to see even more innovative applications of AI in traffic management that will benefit individuals and communities around the world.

## AI-based logistics and delivery

AI-based logistics and delivery are a rapidly growing area of transportation that is changing the way goods are transported and delivered. With the help of AI-powered systems, logistics and delivery can be optimized for speed, efficiency, and sustainability.

AI algorithms can analyze data from various sources, such as traffic patterns, weather, and delivery volume, to optimize delivery routes and schedules. This information can be used to reduce delivery times, minimize transportation costs, and improve the overall customer experience.

AI-based logistics and delivery can also improve the sustainability of transportation systems. By optimizing delivery routes and reducing transportation costs, AI algorithms can reduce emissions and improve environmental sustainability.

AI-based logistics and delivery can also improve the safety of transportation systems. By analyzing data on traffic patterns and accidents, AI algorithms can provide insights into potential hazards and make real-time adjustments to reduce the risk of collisions.

While AI-based logistics and delivery have the potential to bring many benefits to transportation systems and users, there are also important ethical considerations that must be addressed. These include concerns around data privacy, algorithmic bias, and the role of human decision-making in logistics and delivery.

Overall, AI-based logistics and delivery are a rapidly advancing field that has the potential to revolutionize the way goods are transported and delivered. As AI technology continues to improve, we can expect to see even more innovative applications of AI in logistics and delivery that will benefit individuals and communities around the world.

# Chapter 8: Finance

AI technology is transforming the field of finance, providing new ways to manage and invest money, reduce fraud, and improve financial decision-making. AI-powered systems can analyze data from various sources, such as financial statements and market data, to provide insights into investment opportunities and risks.

In this chapter, we will explore the various ways in which AI is transforming finance and how it is enabling individuals and businesses to manage and invest money more effectively. We will examine the impact of AI on financial management, investment strategies, and fraud detection.

We will also discuss the ethical considerations that arise as AI becomes more integrated into finance. While AI has the potential to bring many benefits to individuals and businesses, there are also concerns around data privacy, algorithmic bias, and the role of human decision-making in financial management and investing.

Overall, AI-powered systems are changing the way people manage and invest money, providing new opportunities to reduce risks and increase returns. As AI technology continues to improve, we can expect to see even more innovative applications of AI in finance that will benefit individuals and businesses around the world.

## AI-powered investment strategies

AI-powered investment strategies are a rapidly growing area of finance that is changing the way people invest their money. With the help of AI-powered systems, investment strategies can be optimized for risk and return, and personalized to each individual's unique financial goals and preferences.

AI algorithms can analyze data from various sources, such as financial statements, market data, and news articles, to identify investment opportunities and risks. This information can be used to create personalized investment portfolios that are optimized for each individual's unique financial goals and risk tolerance.

AI-powered investment strategies can also be used to improve the efficiency and effectiveness of investment management. By analyzing large amounts of data in real-time, AI algorithms can identify trends and patterns in financial markets, helping investors make informed decisions.

AI-powered investment strategies can also improve the accessibility of investment opportunities. By providing personalized investment advice and recommendations, AI-powered systems can help individuals who may not have extensive knowledge or experience in finance to make informed investment decisions.

While AI-powered investment strategies have the potential to bring many benefits to investors, there are also important ethical considerations that must be addressed. These include concerns around data privacy, algorithmic bias, and the role of human decision-making in investment strategies.

Overall, AI-powered investment strategies are a rapidly advancing field that has the potential to revolutionize the way people invest their money. As AI technology continues to improve, we can expect to see even more innovative applications of AI in investment strategies that will benefit investors around the world.

## AI-assisted fraud detection

AI-assisted fraud detection is a rapidly growing area of finance that is changing the way financial institutions identify and prevent fraud. With the help of AI-powered systems, financial institutions can analyze large amounts of data in real-time, identify potential fraud, and take action to prevent financial losses.

AI algorithms can analyze data from various sources, such as transaction records and social media, to identify patterns and anomalies that may indicate fraudulent activity. This information can be used to create alerts and flags, which can be reviewed and investigated by human analysts to take action as necessary.

AI-assisted fraud detection can also improve the efficiency and effectiveness of fraud prevention. By automating the detection and reporting of potential fraud, financial institutions can reduce the time and resources required to investigate and prevent fraudulent activity.

AI-assisted fraud detection can also improve the accuracy of fraud detection. By analyzing large amounts of data in real-time, AI algorithms can identify potential fraud that may be difficult for human analysts to detect.

While AI-assisted fraud detection has the potential to bring many benefits to financial institutions and consumers, there are also important ethical considerations that must be addressed. These include concerns around data privacy, algorithmic bias, and the role of human decision-making in fraud detection.

Overall, AI-assisted fraud detection is a rapidly advancing field that has the potential to revolutionize the way financial institutions identify and prevent fraud. As AI technology continues to improve, we can expect to see even more innovative applications of AI in fraud detection that will benefit financial institutions and consumers around the world.

## AI-based financial planning

AI-based financial planning is a rapidly growing area of finance that is changing the way individuals and businesses manage their finances. With the help of AI-powered systems, financial planning can be personalized and optimized to each individual's unique financial goals and circumstances.

AI algorithms can analyze data from various sources, such as income and expense records, investment portfolios, and retirement plans, to create personalized financial plans that are optimized for each individual's unique financial goals and risk tolerance.

AI-based financial planning can also provide insights into potential financial risks and opportunities. By analyzing large amounts of financial data in real-time, AI algorithms can identify potential risks and opportunities, helping individuals and businesses make informed financial decisions.

AI-based financial planning can also improve the accessibility of financial planning services. By providing personalized financial advice and recommendations, AI-powered systems can help individuals who may not have extensive knowledge or experience in finance to make informed financial decisions.

While AI-based financial planning has the potential to bring many benefits to individuals and businesses, there are also important ethical considerations that must be addressed. These include concerns around data privacy, algorithmic bias, and the role of human decision-making in financial planning.

Overall, AI-based financial planning is a rapidly advancing field that has the potential to revolutionize the way people manage their finances. As AI technology continues to improve, we can expect to see even more innovative applications of AI in financial planning that will benefit individuals and businesses around the world.

# Chapter 9: Employment

AI technology is transforming the field of employment, providing new ways to recruit, train, and manage employees. AI-powered systems can analyze data from various sources, such as resumes and job applications, to identify potential candidates for open positions and provide personalized training and development opportunities.

In this chapter, we will explore the various ways in which AI is transforming employment and how it is enabling businesses to manage their workforce more effectively. We will examine the impact of AI on recruitment, training, and performance management.

We will also discuss the ethical considerations that arise as AI becomes more integrated into employment. While AI has the potential to bring many benefits to employers and employees, there are also concerns around data privacy, algorithmic bias, and the impact of AI on job displacement and inequality.

Overall, AI-powered systems are changing the way businesses manage their workforce, providing new opportunities to improve recruitment, training, and performance management. As AI technology continues to improve, we can expect to see even more innovative applications of AI in employment that will benefit employers and employees around the world.

## The impact of AI on job markets

The impact of AI on job markets is a topic of great interest and concern as AI-powered systems become more integrated into the workforce. While AI has the potential to bring many benefits to businesses and employees, there are also concerns around job displacement and the changing nature of work.

AI-powered systems can automate routine tasks and make certain jobs more efficient, but they can also lead to job displacement in industries where automation can replace human labor. This can have a significant impact on workers who may need to retrain or find new employment opportunities.

However, AI can also create new job opportunities in areas such as data science, machine learning, and software engineering. AI can also enhance productivity and enable workers to focus on higher-level tasks that require creativity, problem-solving, and interpersonal skills.

The impact of AI on job markets is also closely tied to issues of inequality and access to education and training. As AI becomes more integrated into the workforce, it is important to ensure that all individuals have access to the necessary education and training to succeed in the changing job market.

Overall, the impact of AI on job markets is complex and multifaceted. While AI has the potential to bring many benefits to businesses and employees, it is important to address concerns around job displacement and inequality and to ensure that all individuals have access to the necessary education and training to succeed in the changing job market.

## AI-assisted recruitment

AI-assisted recruitment is a rapidly growing area of employment that is changing the way businesses identify and hire talent. With the help of AI-powered systems, recruitment can be optimized for efficiency, objectivity, and diversity.

AI algorithms can analyze data from various sources, such as resumes, job applications, and social media, to identify potential candidates for open positions. This information can be used to create personalized candidate profiles that are optimized for each individual job posting.

AI-assisted recruitment can also reduce bias in the hiring process. By removing subjective biases, such as age, gender, and race, AI algorithms can create a more objective and fair hiring process. This can help businesses attract a more diverse pool of candidates and improve the overall quality of their workforce.

AI-assisted recruitment can also improve the efficiency of the hiring process. By automating routine tasks, such as screening resumes and scheduling interviews, AI-powered systems can save time and resources for recruiters and hiring managers.

While AI-assisted recruitment has the potential to bring many benefits to businesses and job seekers, there are also important ethical considerations that must be addressed. These include concerns around data privacy, algorithmic bias, and the role of human decision-making in the hiring process.

Overall, AI-assisted recruitment is a rapidly advancing field that has the potential to revolutionize the way businesses identify and hire talent. As AI technology continues to improve, we can expect to see even more innovative applications of AI in recruitment that will benefit businesses and job seekers around the world.

# AI-powered workplace management

AI-powered workplace management is a rapidly growing area of employment that is changing the way businesses manage their workforce. With the help of AI-powered systems, workplace management can be optimized for efficiency, productivity, and employee well-being.

AI algorithms can analyze data from various sources, such as employee feedback, workplace sensors, and productivity metrics, to provide insights into employee performance and engagement. This information can be used to create personalized employee profiles that are optimized for each individual's unique work style and preferences.

AI-powered workplace management can also improve the efficiency of management tasks. By automating routine tasks, such as scheduling and task assignment, AI-powered systems can save time and resources for managers and enable them to focus on higher-level tasks that require creativity and problem-solving.

AI-powered workplace management can also improve the well-being of employees. By analyzing workplace data, AI algorithms can identify potential areas for improvement, such as reducing stress levels or improving work-life balance. This can help businesses create a more supportive and productive work environment.

While AI-powered workplace management has the potential to bring many benefits to businesses and employees, there are also important ethical considerations that must be addressed. These include concerns around data privacy, algorithmic bias, and the impact of AI on employee autonomy and job satisfaction.

Overall, AI-powered workplace management is a rapidly advancing field that has the potential to revolutionize the way businesses manage their workforce. As AI technology continues to improve, we can expect to see even more innovative applications of AI in workplace management that will benefit businesses and employees around the world.

# Chapter 10: Communication

AI technology is transforming the way people communicate, providing new ways to interact with others and access information. AI-powered systems can analyze language patterns and understand natural language processing, providing new tools to improve communication and streamline information sharing.

In this chapter, we will explore the various ways in which AI is transforming communication and how it is enabling individuals and businesses to communicate more effectively. We will examine the impact of AI on language translation, chatbots, and voice assistants.

We will also discuss the ethical considerations that arise as AI becomes more integrated into communication. While AI has the potential to bring many benefits to communication, there are also concerns around data privacy, algorithmic bias, and the impact of AI on human communication skills.

Overall, AI-powered systems are changing the way people communicate, providing new opportunities to improve language translation, streamline customer service, and enhance the accessibility of information. As AI technology continues to improve, we can expect to see even more innovative applications of AI in communication that will benefit individuals and businesses around the world.

## AI-based natural language processing

AI-based natural language processing (NLP) is a rapidly growing area of communication that is changing the way people interact with technology and each other. With the help of AI-powered systems, NLP can analyze language patterns and understand natural language, providing new tools to improve communication and streamline information sharing.

AI algorithms can analyze data from various sources, such as written or spoken text, to understand the meaning and context behind the words. This information can be used to create personalized communication experiences, such as chatbots and voice assistants, that can respond to human inquiries and requests.

AI-based NLP can also improve language translation. By analyzing the structure and meaning behind sentences in different languages, AI algorithms can provide accurate translations that preserve the original meaning and tone of the text.

AI-based NLP can also improve the accessibility of information. By analyzing large amounts of text in real-time, AI algorithms can identify key information and present it in a more easily digestible format for people with disabilities or language barriers.

While AI-based NLP has the potential to bring many benefits to communication, there are also important ethical considerations that must be addressed. These include concerns around data privacy, algorithmic bias, and the impact of AI on human communication skills.

Overall, AI-based NLP is a rapidly advancing field that has the potential to revolutionize the way people interact with technology and each other. As AI technology continues to improve, we can expect to see even more innovative applications of AI in NLP that will benefit individuals and businesses around the world.

## AI-driven chatbots and voice assistants

AI-driven chatbots and voice assistants are rapidly becoming an essential part of communication for businesses and individuals alike. With the help of AI-powered systems, chatbots and voice assistants can provide personalized, efficient, and accessible customer service and support.

AI algorithms can analyze data from various sources, such as customer inquiries and feedback, to create personalized communication experiences. Chatbots and voice assistants can provide quick responses to common questions, freeing up customer service representatives to focus on more complex issues.

AI-driven chatbots and voice assistants can also improve the accessibility of customer service. By providing 24/7 support and multilingual capabilities, chatbots and voice assistants can provide support to customers around the world and those who may have language barriers.

AI-driven chatbots and voice assistants can also improve customer satisfaction. By providing personalized and efficient support, chatbots and voice assistants can enhance the overall customer experience and create a positive impression of the brand.

While AI-driven chatbots and voice assistants have the potential to bring many benefits to communication, there are also important ethical considerations that must be addressed. These include concerns around data privacy, algorithmic bias, and the impact of AI on human communication skills and job displacement.

Overall, AI-driven chatbots and voice assistants are a rapidly advancing field that has the potential to revolutionize the way businesses and individuals communicate. As AI technology continues to improve, we can expect to see even more innovative applications of AI in chatbots and voice assistants that will benefit businesses and individuals around the world.

## AI-assisted translation and interpretation

AI-assisted translation and interpretation is a rapidly growing area of communication that is changing the way people interact with each other across different languages and cultures. With the help of AI-powered systems, translation and interpretation can be made more accurate, efficient, and accessible.

AI algorithms can analyze data from various sources, such as written or spoken text, to understand the meaning and context behind the words in different languages. This information can be used to provide accurate translations and interpretations that preserve the original meaning and tone of the text.

AI-assisted translation and interpretation can also improve communication across different languages and cultures. By providing real-time translation services, AI-powered systems can help individuals and businesses overcome language barriers and communicate more effectively.

AI-assisted translation and interpretation can also improve the accessibility of information. By analyzing large amounts of text in real-time, AI algorithms can provide accurate translations for people with language barriers, making information more accessible to them.

While AI-assisted translation and interpretation has the potential to bring many benefits to communication, there are also important ethical considerations that must be addressed. These include concerns around data privacy, algorithmic bias, and the impact of AI on the human element of translation and interpretation.

Overall, AI-assisted translation and interpretation is a rapidly advancing field that has the potential to revolutionize the way people communicate across different languages and cultures. As AI technology continues to improve, we can expect to see even more innovative applications of AI in translation and interpretation that will benefit individuals and businesses around the world.

# Chapter 11: Social Media

AI technology is transforming the world of social media, providing new ways to analyze data, automate tasks, and personalize user experiences. AI-powered systems can analyze large amounts of social media data to provide insights into user behavior and preferences, enabling businesses to create more targeted marketing campaigns and personalized user experiences.

In this chapter, we will explore the various ways in which AI is transforming social media and how it is enabling businesses and individuals to communicate and connect more effectively. We will examine the impact of AI on social media advertising, content creation, and user engagement.

We will also discuss the ethical considerations that arise as AI becomes more integrated into social media. While AI has the potential to bring many benefits to social media, there are also concerns around data privacy, algorithmic bias, and the impact of AI on human creativity and expression.

Overall, AI-powered systems are changing the way people interact with social media, providing new opportunities to improve advertising, content creation, and user engagement. As AI technology continues to improve, we can expect to see even more innovative applications of AI in social media that will benefit businesses and individuals around the world.

## AI-powered personalized social media feeds

AI-powered personalized social media feeds are changing the way individuals consume and interact with social media content. With the help of AI-powered systems, social media platforms can provide personalized recommendations and content that is tailored to each individual user's preferences and interests.

AI algorithms can analyze data from various sources, such as user behavior and engagement, to create personalized social media feeds. This information can be used to recommend content that is more relevant and interesting to each user, improving their overall social media experience.

AI-powered personalized social media feeds can also improve user engagement. By providing relevant and interesting content, users are more likely to engage with the content and share it with their networks, increasing the overall reach of the content.

AI-powered personalized social media feeds can also improve the effectiveness of social media advertising. By analyzing user behavior and engagement, AI algorithms can provide more targeted and relevant ads to users, improving the effectiveness of the advertising campaign and reducing ad fatigue for users.

While AI-powered personalized social media feeds have the potential to bring many benefits to social media users and businesses, there are also important ethical considerations that must be addressed. These include concerns around data privacy, algorithmic bias, and the impact of AI on human creativity and expression.

Overall, AI-powered personalized social media feeds are a rapidly advancing field that has the potential to revolutionize the way individuals interact with social media content. As AI technology continues to improve, we can expect to see even more innovative applications of AI in personalized social media feeds that will benefit individuals and businesses around the world.

## AI-driven content moderation

AI-driven content moderation is a rapidly growing area of social media that is changing the way online content is monitored and regulated. With the help of AI-powered systems, social media platforms can automatically detect and remove inappropriate or harmful content, improving the safety and well-being of users.

AI algorithms can analyze data from various sources, such as text and images, to detect inappropriate or harmful content, such as hate speech, bullying, or graphic images. This information can be used to flag the content for review by human moderators, or automatically remove it if it violates platform policies.

AI-driven content moderation can also improve the efficiency and scalability of content moderation. By automating routine tasks, such as flagging inappropriate content, AI-powered systems can save time and resources for human moderators, enabling them to focus on more complex cases that require human judgment.

AI-driven content moderation can also improve the overall quality of social media content. By removing harmful or inappropriate content, social media platforms can create a safer and more enjoyable experience for users, and reduce the potential for negative social and psychological impacts.

While AI-driven content moderation has the potential to bring many benefits to social media users and platforms, there are also important ethical considerations that must be addressed. These include concerns around algorithmic bias, the impact of AI on human creativity and expression, and the potential for censorship or limiting free speech.

Overall, AI-driven content moderation is a rapidly advancing field that has the potential to revolutionize the way online content is monitored and regulated. As AI technology continues to improve, we can expect to see even more innovative applications of AI in content moderation that will benefit social media platforms and users around the world.

## AI-based social media advertising

AI-based social media advertising is a rapidly growing area of social media that is changing the way businesses advertise and target consumers. With the help of AI-powered systems, social media platforms can provide more targeted and personalized advertising to users, improving the effectiveness of advertising campaigns and reducing ad fatigue for users.

AI algorithms can analyze data from various sources, such as user behavior and engagement, to create personalized advertising campaigns. This information can be used to recommend ads that are more relevant and interesting to each user, improving their overall advertising experience.

AI-based social media advertising can also improve the efficiency and effectiveness of advertising campaigns. By automating routine tasks, such as targeting and ad placement, AI-powered systems can save time and resources for advertisers, enabling them to focus on creating high-quality ad content and monitoring campaign performance.

AI-based social media advertising can also improve the return on investment (ROI) for advertisers. By providing more targeted and relevant ads to users, advertisers can improve the likelihood of user engagement and conversion, leading to a higher ROI for the advertising campaign.

While AI-based social media advertising has the potential to bring many benefits to businesses and social media platforms, there are also important ethical considerations that must be addressed. These include concerns around data privacy, algorithmic bias, and the potential for excessive or intrusive advertising.

Overall, AI-based social media advertising is a rapidly advancing field that has the potential to revolutionize the way businesses advertise and target consumers. As AI technology continues to improve, we can expect to see even more innovative applications of AI in social media advertising that will benefit businesses, social media platforms, and users around the world.

# Chapter 12: Shopping

AI technology is transforming the world of shopping, providing new ways to analyze consumer behavior, personalize the shopping experience, and improve the efficiency and effectiveness of e-commerce. AI-powered systems can analyze data from various sources, such as consumer browsing and purchasing behavior, to provide personalized recommendations and targeted marketing campaigns.

In this chapter, we will explore the various ways in which AI is transforming shopping and how it is enabling businesses and individuals to shop more effectively. We will examine the impact of AI on e-commerce platforms, product recommendations, and personalized shopping experiences.

We will also discuss the ethical considerations that arise as AI becomes more integrated into shopping. While AI has the potential to bring many benefits to shopping, there are also concerns around data privacy, algorithmic bias, and the impact of AI on human decision-making and creativity.

Overall, AI-powered systems are changing the way people shop, providing new opportunities to improve the efficiency and effectiveness of e-commerce. As AI technology continues to improve, we can expect to see even more innovative applications of AI in shopping that will benefit businesses and individuals around the world.

## AI-assisted personalized product recommendations

AI-assisted personalized product recommendations are changing the way people shop online. With the help of AI-powered systems, e-commerce platforms can provide personalized recommendations to consumers based on their browsing and purchasing behavior, improving their overall shopping experience and increasing the likelihood of conversion.

AI algorithms can analyze data from various sources, such as consumer browsing history and purchase behavior, to create personalized product recommendations. This information can be used to recommend products that are more relevant and interesting to each consumer, improving their overall shopping experience and increasing the likelihood of conversion.

AI-assisted personalized product recommendations can also improve the efficiency and effectiveness of e-commerce platforms. By providing relevant and targeted recommendations, e-commerce platforms can increase the likelihood of consumer engagement and conversion, leading to a higher return on investment (ROI) for the platform.

AI-assisted personalized product recommendations can also improve the overall shopping experience for consumers. By providing personalized and relevant recommendations, consumers are more likely to find products that meet their needs and preferences, improving their overall satisfaction with the e-commerce platform.

While AI-assisted personalized product recommendations have the potential to bring many benefits to e-commerce platforms and consumers, there are also important ethical considerations that must be addressed. These include concerns around data privacy, algorithmic bias, and the impact of AI on human decision-making and creativity.

Overall, AI-assisted personalized product recommendations are a rapidly advancing field that has the potential to revolutionize the way people shop online. As AI technology continues to improve, we can expect to see even more innovative applications of AI in personalized product recommendations that will benefit e-commerce platforms and consumers around the world.

## AI-driven dynamic pricing

AI-driven dynamic pricing is a rapidly growing area of e-commerce that is changing the way businesses price their products and services. With the help of AI-powered systems, businesses can automatically adjust their prices based on real-time market data and consumer behavior, improving their competitiveness and profitability.

AI algorithms can analyze data from various sources, such as consumer purchasing behavior, competitor pricing, and market trends, to determine the optimal price for a product or service. This information can be used to adjust prices in real-time, improving the competitiveness of the business and increasing the likelihood of conversion.

AI-driven dynamic pricing can also improve the efficiency and effectiveness of pricing strategies. By automating pricing decisions, businesses can save time and resources, enabling them to focus on other areas of the business, such as product development and marketing.

AI-driven dynamic pricing can also benefit consumers. By providing real-time pricing adjustments, consumers can access products and services at a lower price point, increasing the accessibility of the products and services to a wider range of consumers.

While AI-driven dynamic pricing has the potential to bring many benefits to businesses and consumers, there are also important ethical considerations that must be addressed. These include concerns around transparency and fairness in pricing, as well as the potential for price discrimination and exploitation of consumer data.

Overall, AI-driven dynamic pricing is a rapidly advancing field that has the potential to revolutionize the way businesses price their products and services. As AI technology continues to improve, we can expect to see even more innovative applications of AI in dynamic pricing that will benefit businesses and consumers around the world.

## AI-based inventory management

AI-based inventory management is a rapidly growing area of e-commerce that is changing the way businesses manage their inventory levels. With the help of AI-powered systems, businesses can automatically monitor and optimize their inventory levels, improving their efficiency and profitability.

AI algorithms can analyze data from various sources, such as historical sales data, current demand, and market trends, to predict future demand and optimize inventory levels. This information can be used to automate inventory replenishment, reducing the risk of stockouts and overstocking.

AI-based inventory management can also improve the accuracy and efficiency of inventory management. By automating routine inventory management tasks, businesses can save time and resources, enabling them to focus on other areas of the business, such as product development and marketing.

AI-based inventory management can also benefit consumers. By optimizing inventory levels, businesses can ensure that products are always available when consumers need them, improving the overall shopping experience and increasing customer loyalty.

While AI-based inventory management has the potential to bring many benefits to businesses and consumers, there are also important ethical considerations that must be addressed. These include concerns around data privacy and algorithmic bias, as well as the potential impact on small businesses and traditional retail models.

Overall, AI-based inventory management is a rapidly advancing field that has the potential to revolutionize the way businesses manage their inventory levels. As AI technology continues to improve, we can expect to see even more innovative applications of AI in inventory management that will benefit businesses and consumers around the world.

# Chapter 13: Travel

AI technology is transforming the travel industry, providing new ways to analyze consumer behavior, personalize travel experiences, and improve the efficiency and effectiveness of travel planning. AI-powered systems can analyze data from various sources, such as consumer travel preferences, booking behavior, and weather and traffic patterns, to provide personalized recommendations and targeted marketing campaigns.

In this chapter, we will explore the various ways in which AI is transforming travel and how it is enabling businesses and individuals to plan and book travel more effectively. We will examine the impact of AI on travel booking platforms, personalized travel recommendations, and travel itinerary management.

We will also discuss the ethical considerations that arise as AI becomes more integrated into travel. While AI has the potential to bring many benefits to travel, there are also concerns around data privacy, algorithmic bias, and the impact of AI on human decision-making and creativity.

Overall, AI-powered systems are changing the way people travel, providing new opportunities to improve the efficiency and effectiveness of travel planning. As AI technology continues to improve, we can expect to see even more innovative applications of AI in travel that will benefit businesses and individuals around the world.

## AI-powered travel planning

AI-powered travel planning is changing the way people plan and book their travel. With the help of AI-powered systems, travel planning can be made more efficient, personalized and convenient for individuals.

AI algorithms can analyze data from various sources, such as consumer travel preferences, booking behavior, and weather and traffic patterns, to provide personalized travel recommendations. This information can be used to recommend travel destinations, accommodations, and activities that are more relevant and interesting to each traveler, improving their overall travel experience.

AI-powered travel planning can also improve the efficiency and effectiveness of travel planning. By automating routine tasks, such as booking and itinerary management, AI-powered systems can save time and resources for travelers, enabling them to focus on other aspects of their travel, such as packing and sightseeing.

AI-powered travel planning can also benefit the travel industry. By providing more targeted and relevant travel recommendations, travel businesses can increase the likelihood of travel booking and engagement, leading to a higher return on investment (ROI) for the travel industry.

While AI-powered travel planning has the potential to bring many benefits to travelers and the travel industry, there are also important ethical considerations that must be addressed. These include concerns around data privacy, algorithmic bias, and the impact of AI on human decision-making and creativity.

Overall, AI-powered travel planning is a rapidly advancing field that has the potential to revolutionize the way people plan and book their travel. As AI technology continues to improve, we can expect to see even more innovative applications of AI in travel planning that will benefit individuals and the travel industry around the world.

## AI-assisted booking and reservations

AI-assisted booking and reservations are changing the way people make reservations for travel, accommodations, and other services. With the help of AI-powered systems, the booking process can be made more efficient, personalized and convenient for individuals.

AI algorithms can analyze data from various sources, such as consumer booking history and behavior, to provide personalized booking recommendations. This information can be used to recommend available slots, timings, and services that are more relevant and suitable for each individual, improving their overall booking experience.

AI-assisted booking and reservations can also improve the efficiency and effectiveness of the booking process. By automating routine booking tasks, such as availability checks and booking confirmation, AI-powered systems can save time and resources for both individuals and businesses, enabling them to focus on other aspects of their travel and services.

AI-assisted booking and reservations can also benefit the service industry. By providing more targeted and efficient booking services, service businesses can increase the likelihood of customer engagement and satisfaction, leading to a higher return on investment (ROI) for the service industry.

While AI-assisted booking and reservations have the potential to bring many benefits to individuals and service businesses, there are also important ethical considerations that must be addressed. These include concerns around data privacy, algorithmic bias, and the impact of AI on human decision-making and creativity.

Overall, AI-assisted booking and reservations are a rapidly advancing field that has the potential to revolutionize the way people make reservations for travel, accommodations, and other services. As AI technology continues to improve, we can expect to see even more innovative applications of AI in booking and reservations that will benefit individuals and service businesses around the world.

## AI-driven travel recommendations

AI-driven travel recommendations are changing the way people discover and plan their travel experiences. With the help of AI-powered systems, travel recommendations can be made more personalized and tailored to the preferences of each traveler.

AI algorithms can analyze data from various sources, such as travel history, social media activity, and search history, to provide personalized travel recommendations. This information can be used to recommend travel destinations, accommodations, and activities that are more relevant and interesting to each traveler, improving their overall travel experience.

AI-driven travel recommendations can also improve the efficiency and effectiveness of travel planning. By providing relevant and targeted travel recommendations, individuals can save time and resources in researching and planning their travel experiences.

AI-driven travel recommendations can also benefit the travel industry. By providing more personalized and targeted travel recommendations, travel businesses can increase the likelihood of travel booking and engagement, leading to a higher return on investment (ROI) for the travel industry.

While AI-driven travel recommendations have the potential to bring many benefits to travelers and the travel industry, there are also important ethical considerations that must be addressed. These include concerns around data privacy, algorithmic bias, and the impact of AI on human decision-making and creativity.

Overall, AI-driven travel recommendations are a rapidly advancing field that has the potential to revolutionize the way people discover and plan their travel experiences. As AI technology continues to improve, we can expect to see even more innovative applications of AI in travel recommendations that will benefit individuals and the travel industry around the world.

# Chapter 14: Mental Health

AI technology is transforming the field of mental health, providing new ways to diagnose and treat mental health conditions, as well as monitor and support mental health and wellbeing. AI-powered systems can analyze data from various sources, such as patient history, medical records, and behavioral patterns, to provide personalized and effective mental health interventions.

In this chapter, we will explore the various ways in which AI is transforming mental health and how it is enabling individuals to improve their mental health and wellbeing. We will examine the impact of AI on mental health diagnosis, personalized treatment, and mental health monitoring and support.

We will also discuss the ethical considerations that arise as AI becomes more integrated into mental health. While AI has the potential to bring many benefits to mental health, there are also concerns around data privacy, algorithmic bias, and the impact of AI on human decision-making and the therapeutic relationship.

Overall, AI-powered systems are changing the way we approach mental health, providing new opportunities to improve mental health outcomes and support individuals in their mental health journeys. As AI technology continues to improve, we can expect to see even more innovative applications of AI in mental health that will benefit individuals and the mental health field as a whole.

## AI-assisted mental health counseling

AI-assisted mental health counseling is a rapidly growing area of mental health care that is changing the way individuals access mental health support and treatment. With the help of AI-powered systems, mental health counseling can be made more accessible, personalized and effective for individuals.

AI algorithms can analyze data from various sources, such as patient history, medical records, and behavioral patterns, to provide personalized mental health interventions. This information can be used to recommend therapeutic approaches, treatment plans, and coping strategies that are more relevant and effective for each individual, improving their overall mental health outcomes.

AI-assisted mental health counseling can also improve the accessibility of mental health care. By providing virtual mental health counseling and support, individuals can access mental health care from the comfort of their own homes, reducing barriers to care such as distance, transportation, and cost.

AI-assisted mental health counseling can also benefit mental health professionals. By automating routine counseling tasks, such as appointment scheduling and note-taking, AI-powered systems can save time and resources for mental health professionals, enabling them to focus on other aspects of their practice, such as therapeutic interventions and treatment planning.

While AI-assisted mental health counseling has the potential to bring many benefits to individuals and mental health professionals, there are also important ethical considerations that must be addressed. These include concerns around data privacy, algorithmic bias, and the impact of AI on the therapeutic relationship and the quality of mental health care.

Overall, AI-assisted mental health counseling is a rapidly advancing field that has the potential to revolutionize the way we approach mental health care. As AI technology continues to improve, we can expect to see even more innovative applications of AI in mental health counseling that will benefit individuals and mental health professionals around the world.

## AI-powered emotion recognition

AI-powered emotion recognition is a rapidly advancing area of artificial intelligence that is changing the way we understand and respond to human emotions. With the help of AI-powered systems, emotions can be accurately and objectively recognized and classified based on various physiological and behavioral signals.

AI algorithms can analyze data from various sources, such as facial expressions, voice tone, and body language, to detect and recognize different emotions, such as happiness, sadness, anger, and fear. This information can be used to provide personalized and context-specific responses, such as recommending coping strategies or providing emotional support.

AI-powered emotion recognition can have many practical applications in various fields, such as mental health, education, customer service, and security. For example, in mental health, AI-powered emotion recognition can be used to detect and monitor changes in emotional states, providing timely interventions and support for individuals with mental health conditions.

In education, AI-powered emotion recognition can be used to improve the effectiveness of learning by providing real-time feedback on students' emotional engagement and comprehension. In customer service, AI-powered emotion recognition can be used to enhance customer experiences by providing personalized responses based on customers' emotional states.

While AI-powered emotion recognition has the potential to bring many benefits, there are also important ethical considerations that must be addressed. These include concerns around data privacy, algorithmic bias, and the potential for misuse, such as using emotion recognition for surveillance or discriminatory purposes.

Overall, AI-powered emotion recognition is a rapidly advancing field that has the potential to revolutionize the way we understand and respond to human emotions. As AI technology continues to improve, we can expect to see even more innovative applications of AI in emotion recognition that will benefit individuals and various industries around the world.

# AI-based mental health assessment and diagnosis

AI-based mental health assessment and diagnosis is a rapidly advancing area of mental health care that is changing the way we identify and diagnose mental health conditions. With the help of AI-powered systems, mental health assessment and diagnosis can be made more accurate, efficient, and personalized for individuals.

AI algorithms can analyze data from various sources, such as patient history, medical records, and behavioral patterns, to provide more accurate and objective mental health assessments and diagnoses. This information can be used to identify potential mental health conditions, recommend appropriate treatment plans, and monitor treatment progress over time.

AI-based mental health assessment and diagnosis can also improve the efficiency and accessibility of mental health care. By automating routine assessment and diagnosis tasks, such as screening and symptom evaluation, AI-powered systems can save time and resources for mental health professionals and enable more individuals to access mental health care.

AI-based mental health assessment and diagnosis can also benefit mental health professionals. By providing more accurate and objective assessments and diagnoses, AI-powered systems can help mental health professionals make more informed decisions and provide more effective treatments.

While AI-based mental health assessment and diagnosis has the potential to bring many benefits, there are also important ethical considerations that must be addressed. These include concerns around data privacy, algorithmic bias, and the potential for misuse, such as using mental health assessment and diagnosis for discriminatory purposes.

Overall, AI-based mental health assessment and diagnosis is a rapidly advancing field that has the potential to revolutionize the way we identify and diagnose mental health conditions. As AI technology continues to improve, we can expect to see even more innovative applications of AI in mental health assessment and diagnosis that will benefit individuals and mental health professionals around the world.

# Chapter 15: Aging

AI technology is transforming the field of aging, providing new ways to support and improve the lives of older adults. With the global population of older adults rapidly increasing, the use of AI in aging is becoming increasingly important for addressing the complex challenges faced by older adults and their caregivers.

In this chapter, we will explore the various ways in which AI is transforming aging and how it is enabling individuals to age in place, improve their health and wellbeing, and receive better care and support. We will examine the impact of AI on aging-related areas such as healthcare, home automation, transportation, and social connection.

We will also discuss the ethical considerations that arise as AI becomes more integrated into aging. While AI has the potential to bring many benefits to aging, there are also concerns around data privacy, algorithmic bias, and the impact of AI on human decision-making and social relationships.

Overall, AI-powered systems are changing the way we approach aging, providing new opportunities to support and enhance the lives of older adults. As AI technology continues to improve, we can expect to see even more innovative applications of AI in aging that will benefit older adults and their caregivers around the world.

## AI-powered assistive technologies for seniors

AI-powered assistive technologies for seniors are transforming the way older adults age and providing new opportunities for them to live independently, improve their health and wellbeing, and receive better care and support.

AI algorithms can analyze data from various sources, such as medical records, wearable devices, and smart home sensors, to provide personalized and timely support for older adults. This information can be used to monitor health and wellness, provide reminders for medication and appointments, and detect and respond to emergency situations.

AI-powered assistive technologies for seniors can also improve social connection and reduce loneliness. By providing virtual companionship and social support, older adults can maintain connections with friends and family, participate in social activities, and stay engaged with their communities.

AI-powered assistive technologies for seniors can also benefit caregivers and healthcare professionals. By automating routine tasks, such as medication management and health monitoring, AI-powered systems can save time and resources for caregivers and healthcare professionals, enabling them to provide more personalized and effective care.

While AI-powered assistive technologies for seniors have the potential to bring many benefits, there are also important ethical considerations that must be addressed. These include concerns around data privacy, algorithmic bias, and the impact of AI on human decision-making and social relationships.

Overall, AI-powered assistive technologies for seniors are a rapidly advancing field that has the potential to revolutionize the way we support and care for older adults. As AI technology continues to improve, we can expect to see even more innovative applications of AI in assistive technologies for seniors that will benefit older adults, caregivers, and healthcare professionals around the world.

## AI-assisted healthcare for seniors

AI-assisted healthcare for seniors is a rapidly advancing area of healthcare that is changing the way we provide medical care and support to older adults. With the global population of older adults rapidly increasing, the use of AI in healthcare for seniors is becoming increasingly important for addressing the complex healthcare needs of this population.

AI algorithms can analyze data from various sources, such as medical records, wearable devices, and smart home sensors, to provide personalized and timely healthcare support for older adults. This information can be used to monitor health and wellness, detect potential health issues, and recommend appropriate medical interventions.

AI-assisted healthcare for seniors can also improve the efficiency and effectiveness of healthcare delivery. By automating routine healthcare tasks, such as patient monitoring and medication management, AI-powered systems can save time and resources for healthcare professionals and enable them to focus on more complex medical interventions.

AI-assisted healthcare for seniors can also benefit seniors and their families. By providing virtual healthcare support and monitoring, seniors can access medical care and support from the comfort of their own homes, reducing the need for frequent trips to medical facilities and improving their overall quality of life.

While AI-assisted healthcare for seniors has the potential to bring many benefits, there are also important ethical considerations that must be addressed. These include concerns around data privacy, algorithmic bias, and the impact of AI on the human touch in healthcare and the therapeutic relationship.

Overall, AI-assisted healthcare for seniors is a rapidly advancing field that has the potential to revolutionize the way we provide medical care and support to older adults. As AI technology continues to improve, we can expect to see even more innovative applications of AI in healthcare for seniors that will benefit seniors, their families, and healthcare professionals around the world.

## AI-driven home monitoring and safety for seniors

AI-driven home monitoring and safety for seniors is a rapidly growing area of technology that is improving the safety and independence of older adults. With the global population of older adults rapidly increasing, the use of AI in home monitoring and safety is becoming increasingly important for addressing the safety and security needs of this population.

AI algorithms can analyze data from various sources, such as smart home sensors and wearable devices, to detect potential safety risks and provide timely interventions. This information can be used to monitor the health and wellbeing of seniors, detect falls, and identify potential safety hazards in the home.

AI-driven home monitoring and safety for seniors can also improve the efficiency and effectiveness of emergency response. By providing real-time notifications and alerts, emergency responders can be quickly dispatched to the location of a potential emergency, improving response times and outcomes.

AI-driven home monitoring and safety for seniors can also benefit caregivers and family members. By providing remote monitoring and notifications, caregivers and family members can stay informed about the safety and wellbeing of their loved ones, even from a distance.

While AI-driven home monitoring and safety for seniors has the potential to bring many benefits, there are also important ethical considerations that must be addressed. These include concerns around data privacy, algorithmic bias, and the impact of AI on human decision-making and social relationships.

Overall, AI-driven home monitoring and safety for seniors is a rapidly advancing field that has the potential to revolutionize the way we provide safety and security for older adults. As AI technology continues to improve, we can expect to see even more innovative applications of AI in home monitoring and safety for seniors that will benefit seniors, their families, and caregivers around the world.

# Chapter 16: Food

AI technology is transforming the way we produce, distribute, and consume food, providing new opportunities to address food security, reduce waste, and improve the sustainability of our food systems. In this chapter, we will explore the various ways in which AI is transforming the food industry and how it is enabling individuals to make healthier and more sustainable food choices.

We will examine the impact of AI on food-related areas such as agriculture, food production, distribution, and consumption. We will also discuss the ethical considerations that arise as AI becomes more integrated into the food industry, such as concerns around food safety, data privacy, and the potential impact of AI on human decision-making and social relationships.

Overall, AI-powered systems are changing the way we approach food, providing new opportunities to address the challenges of our current food systems and improve the sustainability and health of our food supply. As AI technology continues to improve, we can expect to see even more innovative applications of AI in food that will benefit individuals and communities around the world.

## AI-assisted personalized nutrition planning

AI-assisted personalized nutrition planning is an emerging area of nutrition science that is changing the way we approach diet and nutrition. With the global rise of chronic diseases related to poor dietary habits, AI-assisted personalized nutrition planning has become increasingly important for addressing individual nutritional needs and improving overall health and wellbeing.

AI algorithms can analyze data from various sources, such as medical records, genetic testing, and dietary habits, to provide personalized nutrition plans for individuals. This information can be used to recommend specific dietary interventions based on an individual's unique nutritional needs, preferences, and goals.

AI-assisted personalized nutrition planning can also improve the efficiency and effectiveness of nutrition counseling. By automating routine tasks, such as dietary assessment and meal planning, AI-powered systems can save time and resources for nutrition professionals and enable them to provide more personalized and effective nutritional support.

AI-assisted personalized nutrition planning can also benefit individuals. By providing personalized nutrition plans, individuals can make informed decisions about their dietary habits, improve their nutritional intake, and reduce their risk of chronic diseases related to poor diet.

While AI-assisted personalized nutrition planning has the potential to bring many benefits, there are also important ethical considerations that must be addressed. These include concerns around data privacy, algorithmic bias, and the potential for misuse, such as using personalized nutrition plans for discriminatory purposes.

Overall, AI-assisted personalized nutrition planning is a rapidly advancing field that has the potential to revolutionize the way we approach diet and nutrition. As AI technology continues to improve, we can expect to see even more innovative applications of AI in personalized nutrition planning that will benefit individuals, nutrition professionals, and communities around the world.

## AI-based food delivery services

AI-based food delivery services are transforming the way we order and receive food, providing new opportunities for convenience, speed, and personalization. With the rise of on-demand food delivery services, AI has become increasingly important for improving the efficiency and effectiveness of food delivery operations.

AI algorithms can analyze data from various sources, such as customer orders, traffic patterns, and weather conditions, to optimize food delivery routes, reduce delivery times, and improve customer satisfaction. This information can be used to provide real-time delivery updates to customers and ensure that their orders are delivered promptly and accurately.

AI-based food delivery services can also improve the personalization of food orders. By analyzing customer ordering patterns and preferences, AI-powered systems can provide personalized recommendations and suggestions for food items that customers may enjoy.

AI-based food delivery services can also benefit food businesses. By providing real-time analytics and insights, food businesses can make data-driven decisions to improve their operations and customer experience. Additionally, by optimizing delivery routes and reducing delivery times, food businesses can improve the efficiency and profitability of their delivery operations.

While AI-based food delivery services have the potential to bring many benefits, there are also important ethical considerations that must be addressed. These include concerns around data privacy, algorithmic bias, and the impact of AI on employment in the food delivery industry.

Overall, AI-based food delivery services are a rapidly advancing field that has the potential to revolutionize the way we order and receive food. As AI technology continues to improve, we can expect to see even more innovative applications of AI in food delivery that will benefit customers, food businesses, and delivery professionals around the world.

# AI-powered recipe suggestions and meal planning

AI-powered recipe suggestions and meal planning are transforming the way we approach cooking and meal preparation, providing new opportunities for convenience, creativity, and healthfulness. With the rise of online recipe platforms and meal kit delivery services, AI has become increasingly important for improving the efficiency and effectiveness of meal planning and recipe recommendations.

AI algorithms can analyze data from various sources, such as dietary preferences, nutritional requirements, and ingredient availability, to provide personalized recipe suggestions and meal plans for individuals. This information can be used to recommend specific recipes based on an individual's unique dietary needs, preferences, and goals.

AI-powered recipe suggestions and meal planning can also improve the creativity and variety of meal preparation. By suggesting new and innovative recipe ideas, individuals can expand their culinary horizons and experiment with new ingredients and flavor combinations.

AI-powered recipe suggestions and meal planning can also benefit individuals' health and wellbeing. By recommending recipes that meet nutritional requirements and dietary preferences, individuals can make informed decisions about their dietary habits, improve their nutritional intake, and reduce their risk of chronic diseases related to poor diet.

While AI-powered recipe suggestions and meal planning have the potential to bring many benefits, there are also important ethical considerations that must be addressed. These include concerns around data privacy, algorithmic bias, and the potential for misuse, such as using personalized meal plans for discriminatory purposes.

Overall, AI-powered recipe suggestions and meal planning are a rapidly advancing field that has the potential to revolutionize the way we approach cooking and meal preparation. As AI technology continues to improve, we can expect to see even more innovative applications of AI in recipe suggestions and meal planning that will benefit individuals, food businesses, and communities around the world.

# Chapter 17: Environment

AI technology is transforming the way we approach environmental sustainability, providing new opportunities to address the complex and pressing environmental challenges facing our world. In this chapter, we will explore the various ways in which AI is transforming the environmental sector and how it is enabling individuals and organizations to make more informed decisions and take more effective actions to protect our planet.

We will examine the impact of AI on environmental areas such as climate change, energy management, waste reduction, and biodiversity conservation. We will also discuss the ethical considerations that arise as AI becomes more integrated into the environmental sector, such as concerns around data privacy, algorithmic bias, and the potential impact of AI on human decision-making and social relationships.

Overall, AI-powered systems are changing the way we approach environmental sustainability, providing new opportunities to address the challenges of our current environmental systems and improve the health and wellbeing of our planet. As AI technology continues to improve, we can expect to see even more innovative applications of AI in environmental sustainability that will benefit individuals, organizations, and communities around the world.

## AI-driven climate modeling and prediction

AI-driven climate modeling and prediction is an emerging area of climate science that is changing the way we understand and address the impacts of climate change. With the global rise in greenhouse gas emissions and the increasing severity of climate-related disasters, AI-assisted climate modeling and prediction has become increasingly important for improving our ability to adapt to and mitigate the impacts of climate change.

AI algorithms can analyze large amounts of data from various sources, such as satellite imagery, weather data, and climate models, to provide more accurate and detailed predictions of future climate patterns and trends. This information can be used to inform policy decisions, support disaster preparedness and response efforts, and guide climate adaptation and mitigation strategies.

AI-driven climate modeling and prediction can also improve the efficiency and effectiveness of climate research. By automating routine tasks, such as data processing and analysis, AI-powered systems can save time and resources for climate researchers and enable them to focus on more complex and innovative research questions.

AI-driven climate modeling and prediction can also benefit individuals and communities. By providing more accurate and reliable climate information, individuals and communities can make more informed decisions about how to prepare for and respond to climate-related disasters, reduce their carbon footprint, and support climate adaptation and mitigation efforts.

While AI-driven climate modeling and prediction has the potential to bring many benefits, there are also important ethical considerations that must be addressed. These include concerns around data privacy, algorithmic bias, and the potential for misuse, such as using climate predictions for discriminatory purposes.

Overall, AI-driven climate modeling and prediction is a rapidly advancing field that has the potential to revolutionize the way we understand and address the impacts of climate change. As AI technology continues to improve, we can expect to see even more innovative applications of AI in climate modeling and prediction that will benefit individuals, organizations, and communities around the world.

## AI-assisted environmental monitoring and conservation

AI-assisted environmental monitoring and conservation is a rapidly advancing field that is changing the way we approach environmental sustainability, providing new opportunities for more effective and efficient monitoring and conservation efforts. With the global rise in environmental degradation and biodiversity loss, AI-powered systems have become increasingly important for improving our ability to protect and preserve our natural resources.

AI algorithms can analyze large amounts of data from various sources, such as satellite imagery, sensor networks, and field observations, to provide real-time monitoring and analysis of environmental conditions and ecosystem health. This information can be used to inform conservation efforts, support environmental policy decisions, and guide sustainable development.

AI-assisted environmental monitoring and conservation can also improve the efficiency and effectiveness of environmental conservation efforts. By automating routine tasks, such as data collection and analysis, AI-powered systems can save time and resources for conservation professionals and enable them to focus on more complex and innovative conservation strategies.

AI-assisted environmental monitoring and conservation can also benefit individuals and communities. By providing more accurate and detailed environmental information, individuals and communities can make more informed decisions about their impact on the environment, and support conservation efforts in their local communities.

While AI-assisted environmental monitoring and conservation has the potential to bring many benefits, there are also important ethical considerations that must be addressed. These include concerns around data privacy, algorithmic bias, and the potential for misuse, such as using environmental data for discriminatory purposes.

Overall, AI-assisted environmental monitoring and conservation is a promising area of environmental science that has the potential to revolutionize the way we protect and preserve our natural resources. As AI technology continues to improve, we can expect to see even more innovative applications of AI in environmental monitoring and conservation that will benefit individuals, organizations, and communities around the world.

## AI-based sustainability planning and decision-making

AI-based sustainability planning and decision-making is an emerging field that is changing the way we approach sustainable development, providing new opportunities for more informed and effective sustainability planning and decision-making. With the global rise in environmental degradation and climate change, AI-powered systems have become increasingly important for improving our ability to address these complex and pressing environmental challenges.

AI algorithms can analyze large amounts of data from various sources, such as environmental sensors, climate models, and social media platforms, to provide insights and recommendations for sustainable development and decision-making. This information can be used to inform policy decisions, guide sustainable urban planning, and support environmentally responsible business practices.

AI-based sustainability planning and decision-making can also improve the efficiency and effectiveness of sustainability efforts. By automating routine tasks, such as data collection and analysis, AI-powered systems can save time and resources for sustainability professionals and enable them to focus on more complex and innovative sustainability strategies.

AI-based sustainability planning and decision-making can also benefit individuals and communities. By providing more accurate and detailed information on sustainable development, individuals and communities can make more informed decisions about their impact on the environment, and support sustainable development efforts in their local communities.

While AI-based sustainability planning and decision-making has the potential to bring many benefits, there are also important ethical considerations that must be addressed. These include concerns around data privacy, algorithmic bias, and the potential for misuse, such as using sustainability data for discriminatory purposes.

Overall, AI-based sustainability planning and decision-making is a promising area of sustainable development that has the potential to revolutionize the way we approach environmental sustainability. As AI technology continues to improve, we can expect to see even more innovative applications of AI in sustainability planning and decision-making that will benefit individuals, organizations, and communities around the world.

# Chapter 18: Sports

AI technology is transforming the world of sports, providing new opportunities for improving performance, enhancing fan experiences, and advancing athlete safety. In this chapter, we will explore the various ways in which AI is transforming the sports industry and how it is enabling athletes, coaches, and fans to achieve new levels of success and enjoyment.

We will examine the impact of AI on sports areas such as training and performance analysis, fan engagement and experiences, and athlete safety and injury prevention. We will also discuss the ethical considerations that arise as AI becomes more integrated into the sports industry, such as concerns around data privacy, algorithmic bias, and the potential impact of AI on athletic integrity and fairness.

Overall, AI-powered systems are changing the way we approach sports, providing new opportunities to improve athletic performance, enhance fan experiences, and advance athlete safety. As AI technology continues to improve, we can expect to see even more innovative applications of AI in sports that will benefit athletes, fans, and sports organizations around the world.

## AI-powered sports analytics

AI-powered sports analytics is a rapidly growing area of sports technology that is transforming the way we understand and analyze athletic performance. With the vast amounts of data available in sports, AI-assisted analytics can provide insights and recommendations that were previously unattainable.

AI algorithms can analyze large amounts of data from various sources, such as player stats, game footage, and physiological data, to provide real-time insights into athlete performance and team strategies. This information can be used to inform coaching decisions, player development, and game planning.

AI-powered sports analytics can also benefit fans and sports organizations. By providing more accurate and detailed analysis of player and team performance, fans can gain a deeper understanding of the game and engage with sports in new and exciting ways. Sports organizations can use AI-powered analytics to improve player scouting, enhance team strategies, and make more informed decisions about player contracts and team investments.

AI-powered sports analytics can also improve athlete safety and injury prevention. By analyzing player movement patterns and biomechanical data, AI-assisted analytics can identify potential injury risks and provide insights into injury prevention strategies.

While AI-powered sports analytics has the potential to bring many benefits, there are also important ethical considerations that must be addressed. These include concerns around data privacy, algorithmic bias, and the potential for misuse, such as using sports data for discriminatory purposes.

Overall, AI-powered sports analytics is a promising area of sports technology that has the potential to revolutionize the way we understand and analyze athletic performance. As AI technology continues to improve, we can expect to see even more innovative applications of AI in sports analytics that will benefit athletes, coaches, and sports organizations around the world.

## AI-assisted sports training and coaching

AI-assisted sports training and coaching is an innovative application of AI technology that is transforming the way athletes train and improve their skills. With the ability to analyze vast amounts of data and provide real-time feedback, AI-powered training and coaching can help athletes achieve new levels of performance.

AI algorithms can analyze data from various sources, such as video footage and biometric sensors, to provide personalized feedback and recommendations for improving athletic technique and performance. This information can be used by coaches to develop individualized training plans that focus on areas where athletes need the most improvement.

AI-assisted sports training and coaching can also benefit athletes by providing new opportunities for remote coaching and training. With the ability to analyze data and provide feedback in real-time, athletes can receive coaching and training from experts around the world, without the need for in-person coaching.

AI-assisted sports training and coaching can also improve athlete safety and injury prevention. By analyzing biomechanical data and identifying potential injury risks, AI-powered systems can provide recommendations for injury prevention strategies and help athletes avoid injuries.

While AI-assisted sports training and coaching has the potential to bring many benefits, there are also important ethical considerations that must be addressed. These include concerns around data privacy, algorithmic bias, and the potential impact of AI on athletic integrity and fairness.

Overall, AI-assisted sports training and coaching is a promising area of sports technology that has the potential to revolutionize the way athletes train and improve their skills. As AI technology continues to improve, we can expect to see even more innovative applications of AI in sports training and coaching that will benefit athletes, coaches, and sports organizations around the world.

## AI-driven sports broadcasting and commentary

AI-driven sports broadcasting and commentary is an innovative application of AI technology that is transforming the way we watch and enjoy sports. With the ability to analyze vast amounts of data in real-time, AI-powered broadcasting and commentary can provide fans with a more immersive and personalized viewing experience.

AI algorithms can analyze data from various sources, such as player stats, game footage, and social media feeds, to provide real-time insights and commentary during live sports events. This information can be used to create customized graphics, highlight reels, and statistical analysis that enhance the fan experience.

AI-driven sports broadcasting and commentary can also benefit sports organizations by providing new opportunities for fan engagement and revenue generation. With the ability to personalize content and deliver targeted advertising, sports organizations can increase fan engagement and drive revenue growth.

AI-driven sports broadcasting and commentary can also improve the accuracy and fairness of sports coverage. By using AI to analyze game footage and identify controversial or questionable calls, broadcasters and officials can make more informed decisions and ensure the integrity of the game.

While AI-driven sports broadcasting and commentary has the potential to bring many benefits, there are also important ethical considerations that must be addressed. These include concerns around data privacy, algorithmic bias, and the potential impact of AI on the role of human commentators and broadcasters.

Overall, AI-driven sports broadcasting and commentary is a promising area of sports technology that has the potential to revolutionize the way we watch and enjoy sports. As AI technology continues to improve, we can expect to see even more innovative applications of AI in sports broadcasting and commentary that will enhance the fan experience and benefit sports organizations around the world.

# Chapter 19: Personal Productivity

AI technology is changing the way we approach personal productivity, providing new opportunities for individuals to improve their efficiency and effectiveness in their personal and professional lives. In this chapter, we will explore the various ways in which AI is transforming personal productivity and how it is enabling individuals to achieve new levels of success and productivity.

We will examine the impact of AI on personal productivity areas such as time management, task organization, and workflow optimization. We will also discuss the ethical considerations that arise as AI becomes more integrated into personal productivity tools, such as concerns around data privacy and the potential for misuse of personal data.

Overall, AI-powered systems are changing the way we approach personal productivity, providing new opportunities to improve our efficiency and effectiveness in our personal and professional lives. As AI technology continues to improve, we can expect to see even more innovative applications of AI in personal productivity that will benefit individuals around the world.

## AI-based task management and scheduling

AI-based task management and scheduling is a promising area of personal productivity that is transforming the way we manage our time and organize our tasks. With the ability to analyze vast amounts of data and provide real-time insights, AI-powered task management and scheduling tools can help individuals optimize their workflow and achieve greater productivity.

AI algorithms can analyze data from various sources, such as calendar events, emails, and to-do lists, to provide personalized recommendations for task prioritization and scheduling. This information can be used to develop individualized task lists and scheduling plans that help individuals stay focused on their most important tasks and achieve their goals.

AI-based task management and scheduling tools can also benefit individuals by providing new opportunities for automation and delegation. With the ability to identify repetitive and time-consuming tasks, AI-powered systems can automate these tasks or delegate them to others, freeing up time for more important tasks.

AI-based task management and scheduling can also improve individual well-being and work-life balance. By providing personalized recommendations for scheduling and task prioritization, individuals can achieve greater productivity while also reducing stress and maintaining a healthy work-life balance.

While AI-based task management and scheduling has the potential to bring many benefits, there are also important ethical considerations that must be addressed. These include concerns around data privacy, algorithmic bias, and the potential for misuse, such as using personal data for discriminatory purposes.

Overall, AI-based task management and scheduling is a promising area of personal productivity that has the potential to revolutionize the way we manage our time and organize our tasks. As AI technology continues to improve, we can expect to see even more innovative applications of AI in task management and scheduling that will benefit individuals around the world.

# AI-assisted email and communication management

AI-assisted email and communication management is a rapidly growing area of personal productivity that is transforming the way we manage our digital communications. With the vast amount of email and communication we receive daily, AI-powered email and communication management tools can help individuals optimize their communication workflow and achieve greater productivity.

AI algorithms can analyze data from various sources, such as email content, sender behavior, and communication patterns, to provide personalized recommendations for email prioritization, organization, and response. This information can be used to develop individualized email management plans that help individuals stay focused on their most important communications and achieve their goals.

AI-assisted email and communication management can also benefit individuals by providing new opportunities for automation and delegation. With the ability to identify repetitive and time-consuming communication tasks, AI-powered systems can automate these tasks or delegate them to others, freeing up time for more important communication tasks.

AI-assisted email and communication management can also improve individual well-being and work-life balance. By providing personalized recommendations for communication prioritization and organization, individuals can achieve greater productivity while also reducing stress and maintaining a healthy work-life balance.

While AI-assisted email and communication management has the potential to bring many benefits, there are also important ethical considerations that must be addressed. These include concerns around data privacy, algorithmic bias, and the potential for misuse, such as using personal data for discriminatory purposes.

Overall, AI-assisted email and communication management is a promising area of personal productivity that has the potential to revolutionize the way we manage our digital communications. As AI technology continues to improve, we can expect to see even more innovative applications of AI in email and communication management that will benefit individuals around the world.

## AI-driven personal assistant apps

AI-driven personal assistant apps are becoming increasingly popular as a means of enhancing personal productivity and organization. These apps use AI algorithms to analyze data from various sources, such as calendar events, emails, and to-do lists, to provide personalized recommendations for task prioritization, scheduling, and communication management.

Personal assistant apps can also assist with daily activities such as making reservations, setting reminders, and finding information online. By using natural language processing and machine learning, these apps can understand complex commands and respond with helpful recommendations and actions.

AI-driven personal assistant apps can also benefit individuals by providing new opportunities for automation and delegation. With the ability to identify repetitive and time-consuming tasks, personal assistant apps can automate these tasks or delegate them to others, freeing up time for more important tasks.

Personal assistant apps can also improve individual well-being and work-life balance. By providing personalized recommendations for task prioritization and scheduling, individuals can achieve greater productivity while also reducing stress and maintaining a healthy work-life balance.

While AI-driven personal assistant apps have the potential to bring many benefits, there are also important ethical considerations that must be addressed. These include concerns around data privacy, algorithmic bias, and the potential for misuse, such as using personal data for discriminatory purposes.

Overall, AI-driven personal assistant apps are a promising area of personal productivity that has the potential to revolutionize the way we manage our daily tasks and activities. As AI technology continues to improve, we can expect to see even more innovative applications of AI in personal assistant apps that will benefit individuals around the world.

# Chapter 20: Conclusion

Artificial intelligence (AI) is transforming our personal lives in numerous ways, from healthcare and fitness to education and entertainment. AI is providing new opportunities to enhance personal productivity, optimize our workflow, and improve our overall quality of life.

In this book, we have explored the various ways in which AI is changing our personal lives, examining the impact of AI on areas such as healthcare, fitness, education, home automation, entertainment, transportation, finance, employment, communication, social media, shopping, travel, mental health, aging, food, environment, sports, and personal productivity.

We have seen how AI-powered technologies and tools are providing new opportunities for individuals to achieve greater efficiency, effectiveness, and success in their personal and professional lives. We have also discussed the ethical considerations that arise as AI becomes more integrated into our daily lives, including concerns around data privacy, algorithmic bias, and the potential for misuse.

As AI technology continues to evolve and improve, we can expect to see even more innovative applications of AI in our personal lives. It is important that we continue to monitor and address the ethical implications of AI, while also embracing the potential benefits that AI can bring to our lives.

In conclusion, the future of AI in our personal lives is exciting and full of potential. As we continue to explore the possibilities of AI, we must remain mindful of the ethical considerations and work towards harnessing the power of AI to create a better world for all.

## A summary of the impact of AI on personal lives

Artificial intelligence (AI) is transforming our personal lives in numerous ways. AI-powered technologies and tools are providing new opportunities for individuals to achieve greater efficiency, effectiveness, and success in areas such as healthcare, fitness, education, home automation, entertainment, transportation, finance, employment, communication, social media, shopping, travel, mental health, aging, food, environment, sports, and personal productivity.

Some specific examples of how AI is impacting personal lives include AI-powered medical diagnosis, AI-assisted surgeries, AI-based personalized workout plans, AI-driven self-driving cars, AI-assisted mental health counseling, AI-assisted recruitment, AI-powered sports analytics, and AI-driven climate modeling and prediction.

While AI is bringing many benefits to our personal lives, there are also important ethical considerations that must be addressed, such as concerns around data privacy, algorithmic bias, and the potential for misuse. As AI technology continues to evolve and improve, it is important that we monitor and address these ethical implications while also embracing the potential benefits that AI can bring to our lives.

**Future possibilities and ethical considerations.**

The future possibilities of AI in our personal lives are vast and exciting. As AI technology continues to evolve and improve, we can expect to see even more innovative applications of AI in areas such as healthcare, fitness, education, home automation, entertainment, transportation, finance, employment, communication, social media, shopping, travel, mental health, aging, food, environment, sports, and personal productivity.

Some potential future possibilities of AI in personal lives include AI-powered virtual reality experiences, AI-driven personalized healthcare, AI-based natural language processing for communication, AI-assisted decision-making in finance and business, and AI-assisted sustainability planning.

However, with the increasing integration of AI into our personal lives, it is important to consider and address the ethical implications of this technology. Some ethical considerations include concerns around data privacy, algorithmic bias, and the potential for misuse, such as using personal data for discriminatory purposes.

It is important that we work towards harnessing the power of AI to create a better world for all while also ensuring that the technology is developed and used in a way that is ethical, transparent, and beneficial to society as a whole. This requires ongoing monitoring and regulation of AI technology and its applications, as well as continued research and discussion around ethical considerations related to AI.

## Final Thoughts

Artificial intelligence (AI) is transforming our personal lives in countless ways, offering new opportunities for productivity, organization, and optimization. The applications of AI in areas such as healthcare, education, entertainment, transportation, and more are vast and constantly evolving. However, it is important to consider the ethical implications of AI, including concerns around data privacy, algorithmic bias, and the potential for misuse.

As we move forward with the integration of AI into our personal lives, we must remain vigilant in addressing these ethical considerations while also embracing the potential benefits that AI can bring. By doing so, we can harness the power of AI to create a better world for all, improving the quality of life for individuals around the globe.